DON'T BOOK A JUDGE BY HIS COVER

DON'T BOOK A JUDGE BY HIS COVER

*A Collection of the World's
Most Outrageous Puns*

Theodore A. Brett

FITHIAN PRESS
Santa Barbara
1990

Library of Congress Cataloging-in-Publication Data

Brett, Theodore A., 1947—
Don't book a judge by his cover:
a collection of the world's most outrageous puns
Theodore A. Brett.
p. cm.
ISBN 0-931832-38-1
1. Puns and punning.
2. American wit and humor.
I. Title.
PN6231.P8B74 1990
818'.5402--dc20   89-27193/CIP

Published by

FITHIAN PRESS
Post Office Box 1525
Santa Barbara, California 93102

DEDICATION

To my children:

To Page, who can find humor in anything, except when the Chicago Cubs are losing;

To Jeremy, who can find humor in absolutely anything.

ACKNOWLEDGMENTS

It is impossible to acknowledge all the contributors of these stories, just as it is impossible to thank everybody who supported this published effort.

Needless to say, appreciation is extended to those nameless many who have related their favorite puns over the years. My parents, Dr. Wilbur and Bernice Brett, were undoubtedly the first to instill in me a love of language and humor. However, when one tries to recall where a particular pun or story was first heard, little but cobwebs and blurred associations emerge, especially when trying to recollect them over twenty years or so. Certain names do sneak through the memory lapses: Burt Skelley, Bob Wilson, Susan Smith, Nancy Webb, Ed Callary, Bill Zeigler, Gay Davidson, Jeremy Brett, Jim Grinnell, Bill Thomlinson, and Beth Thomlinson.

Others whose contributions to this book made it possible include my brother Sam Brett and my sister Erika Brett-Webber. Still others who deserve special thanks include Lynne Kelter, Patricia Greene, Valerie Schwontkowski, Carroll Briggs, Mark Goodkin, Diana Cook, Mary Hagins, Maryjane Paulsen, Chris Kightly, Bob Scettrini, Karla Andersen, Brad and Lanora Mueller, Martin and Kathy Cohn, Ismail and Sally Said, Bill and Phannee Ball, Ed and Jean Callary, and Randy Ruddach.

Special thanks go to John Daniel, Fithian Press publisher. His enthusiasm and support, professional editing, and spirited contributions to the contents and titles of the stories made the entire book possible.

Finally, heartfelt and loving appreciation goes to Beth Thomlinson, whose enthusiasm for this project rivaled and often surpassed my own. Her careful and concerned editing, confidence, and unabashed excitement were critical to getting this book into its final form.

FOREWORD

I don't know when I heard my first pun. I do know that I probably didn't understand it. That may have been the most wondrous thing about it. The intricate linguistic gymnastics that pervade every pun in this book quickly began to fascinate me, and I trust you will derive the same "anguished" pleasure that I do when I hear or read them. The imagination and creativity that turn a familiar expression into something "exquisitely clever" fascinate not only those of us with a love of language, but also those of us who detect that just in our understanding of the pun we are somehow "in on something" almost cryptic. And our pleasure is heightened.

The first pun was probably uttered about twenty minutes after the first human being discovered the magic of language. The ancient Greeks took time out from their fledgling experiments in democracy and geometry. I can picture the architect of the Parthenon gazing with wonder at his geometric perfection and suggesting, "I love my wife but oh, Euclid."

Cleopatra, entangled in her love affairs with Julius Caesar and Marc Antony and watching her beloved Egyptian empire crumble, chose suicide. It was a remarkable example of her tenacity that she managed to find a snake with which to poison herself. Apparently asps were not easy to breed in ancient Egypt. After all, they were adders, not multipliers.

Shakespeare's plays are replete with puns. The Elizabethans, no doubt, eventually grew tired of them, and Shakespeare was briefly imprisoned. Historical records indicate that he was barred on Avon.

We've titled this volume *Don't Book a Judge by His Cover: A Collection of the World's Most Outrageous Puns,* and the key word here is "outrageous." These puns are more than just the punch lines; the puns' outrageousness depends as much on their equally outrageous stories that build up to the punch lines.

These puns have been collected for years. Most were remembered from long-forgotten punsters; others were read and remembered over many years—their origins lost as they passed into the folklore of language. Nobody owns them. They are in the public domain to be enjoyed by all. Some of them are printed here for the first time; others have been reprinted and circulated every time a new collection of jokes and puns came out. They will continue to be rediscovered and enjoyed. These constitute my favorites— at least my favorites among those I remember.

Many hundreds more must be out there, perhaps begging to be printed and distributed. We plan another edition of puns, and your contributions are more than welcome. If you have any of your own outrageous puns and would like to see them printed in a forthcoming collection, send them to me care of Fithian Press, P.O. Box 1525, Santa Barbara, CA 93102. I look forward to reading and enjoying them, and I know others will also.

Ted Brett

CONTENTS

DON'T BOOK A JUDGE BY HIS COVER

SPIES OF LIFE

During the most intense days of the cold war, the Central Intelligence Agency undertook a recruitment drive to bolster its ranks and try to rectify the Russian intelligence advantages. During the initial interviews, two candidates appeared particularly promising. Wayne and Amber were a brother and sister team. Although their fervor and patriotism couldn't be denied and their aptitude for spying was peerless, their one flaw was their inability to get along with each other. Rarely did a moment go by when they weren't arguing, bickering, or insulting each other.

As unorthodox as this behavior may have been, they were admitted to the CIA's training program and both excelled in all their training. However, throughout their training they were constantly arguing and screaming at each other. Their first assignment was to infiltrate a group of Russian agents who were using Washington's nightclubs and restaurants as meeting places to plan their activities. Wayne and Amber had to become familiar with the comings and goings of these restaurants' patrons. One night they had to visit five restaurants in a row.

In order to protect their covers, they had to fit in with the restaurant crowd; that meant drinking and dining as legitimate patrons at these elegant eating establishments. As they went from restaurant to restaurant, they argued, bickered, and screamed at each other, all the while eating full meals and drinking their fill.

Because this was their first assignment, they were observed by a couple of CIA veterans. The observers were amazed at their huge appetites but did witness their arguing. One observer turned to the other and said, "They're dutiful, voracious spies, but Amber raves at Wayne."

A SHORT STORY

In Eastern Europe during the final days of World War II, when the Germans were being forced out of Czechoslovakia, a young man who had worked for the Czech underground was forced to flee for his life. He had been a successful agent, having gotten away many times because of his youth and his size—he was barely five feet tall.

He managed to escape from Prague and tried to make his way across Czechoslovakia to Austria. Finally, having crossed the border, he came to a farmhouse. Exhausted and hungry, and needing to be hidden from the pursuing Germans, he knocked on the door and said, "The Germans are after me; can you cache a small Czech?"

ANOTHER SHORT STORY

I heard this story while vacationing recently in Jamaica. A group of American dwarfs and midgets were holding their annual convention at the same resort, and they realized as never before that they were truly living in a world designed for larger people. The furniture, beds, cabinets, and fixtures were either too large or too tall for their comfort.

They resolved that this would never happen again at one of their conventions. They ran a lottery, conducted raffles, and collected enough money to build their own resort for future meetings—a resort designed for midgets and dwarfs. Of course, some of the rooms would be normal sized for normal-sized people in order to attract as many people as possible to the vacation retreat.

However, special rooms would have smaller accoutrements. Rooms, furniture, fixtures...everything would be smaller for the smaller guests. Futhermore, they resolved that all dwarfs could stay there without paying anything.

They called these rooms stay-free mini pads.

TEA FOR TOOTH

Sri Lanka, formerly Ceylon, is known for its exquisite teas. Colombo, the capital, is the Mecca for tea lovers throughout the world. A self-proclaimed "tea expert" visited Sri Lanka in search of the perfect new tea, a tea he'd never tasted before. Having travelled the world in search of teas, he'd sampled just about all of them. He went into the leading tea emporium and asked for their newest, rarest tea.

The proprietor mentioned Darjeeling teas. "No, I've had Darjeeling all over the world," replied the tea connoisseur. "How about Ginsing?" asked the helpful proprietor. "No, I've had that many times," the expert replied. The owner suggested several other teas—rare, wonderful teas—and the expert replied he'd had all of them, many times.

Finally the owner of the tea emporium told him he had something new: "a rare tea, brewed not from the traditional tea leaves, but from the body of the koala bear known to live only on the Mercy islands just north of New Zealand. This is not the common koala of Australia, but the rare koala from the Mercy Islands." Excited about the prospect of sampling a new tea, the connoisseur sat back and waited in anticipation. Ten minutes later, the proprietor returned with a huge, black, bubbling cauldron and placed it in front of his customer. The tea expert peered in and saw a koala bear floating in the tea. The whole koala—hair, bones, gristle, head...everything.

"I can't drink this," he said, "it's got hair, bones, skin...the whole animal in it."

"Ah, you must remember, sir," said the proprietor, "the koala tea of Mercy is not strained."

ARABIAN FLIGHTS

During the Turkish occupation of the Arabian Peninsula, an Arab spy was captured by the Turks. He managed to escape, but his escape was soon discovered, and the Turks, led by a frantic general, set out to find their prisoner.

The Arab tried to hide out in the tower of a castle, but he discovered a family living there already, and they were about to cook their dinner. He asked them not to give away his hideout, but they insisted on cooking their meal. The smoke from the fire alerted the Turks, and the general led his army to the castle's tower, where the Arab spy was captured.

A lesson to others in this position: Warning—the searching general says that ziggurat smoking can be harmful to your stealth.

FROG GOODNESS SAKE

If you've ever had to go into a bank to try to get a loan, you know how difficult it can be when your income is low...or non-existent. Imagine how difficult it is when you have no job and you're a frog!

One day, a frog went into a local bank to try to arrange a loan. He talked to the loan officer, Mrs. Patricia Wack. When she asked if he had any income, the frog had to say that he had none. He didn't anticipate any, either (apparently there were no inheritances or lotteries at the pond). Finally, Mrs. Patricia Wack asked if he had any collateral. When the frog asked what that was, Wack said it was something of value the bank could hold in case the frog defaulted on the loan.

The frog returned to his pond, rooted around the lily pads, and returned to the bank with a large, white porcelain elephant (it had been in the family for years, just gathering algae). He asked Mrs. Wack if that would serve as collateral. She didn't know, and she took the matter up with the bank president.

"This frog came in with this white porcelain elephant, and he wants to know if he can use it as collateral on a loan," said Mrs. Wack.

The president looked the elephant over and said, "It's a knickknack, Patty Wack, give the frog a loan."

GET IT OFF YOUR CHESS

A few years ago, a world championship chess tournament was being held in New York City. The importance of the tournament was such that, even after most of the challengers had been eliminated, they stayed around in the hotel lobby, talking about their own mighty victories and adventures in the highly competitive world of international chess.

Story after story was spun in the hotel lobby, as each tried to outdo the other with tales of his prowess at the chess table. Finally, the hotel manager had to ask them to stop. The commotion in the lobby was too great; and besides, he said, "I hate to hear chess nuts boasting in an open foyer."

THREE PIECE SUITORS

The chief of an Indian tribe in western Nebraska was faced with a dilemma. He had three daughters. The oldest was one of the most beautiful women who ever lived. She was smart as well as beautiful. The second daughter was also very beautiful, but not quite as striking as the first. The third was very, very plain. (This tribe must have been a group of Plains Indians.)

There were three young Indian warriors vying for the affections of the chief's daughters. To solve the dilemma and get his daughters married, the chief proposed that the three Indian braves go out into the forest and return with evidence of their hunting prowess. All three braves agreed.

The first Indian, the best hunter and warrior in the tribe, immediately spotted a ferocious mountain lion. Taking his bow and arrow, he shot the lion, skinned it, and returned to the Indian camp with the pelt. The chief was impressed, and he asked the young hunter if he wanted to marry his oldest, most beautiful, most accomplished daughter. The brave replied that he did. The chief said, "Take your lion skin to your tepee, lay it on the ground, and my daughter will join you. Then you may consummate your marriage, and tomorrow, with all the rites and traditions of the tribe, I shall perform the sacred marriage ceremony." The young Indian did as he was directed.

The second Indian, not as lucky as the first, took two days to find prey worth shooting to prove his hunting prowess. He spotted a bear. He shot it with his bow and arrow, skinned it, and returned to camp with the bearskin. The chief was impressed, and he asked him if he wanted to marry his second daughter. The brave replied that he did. The chief said, "Take the bearskin to your tepee, lay the pelt on the ground, and my daughter will join you. Then you may consummate your marriage, and tomorrow, in all the rites and traditions of our tribe, I'll perform the sacred marriage ceremony." The Indian did as he was directed.

The third Indian brave was, to be frank, a bumbling, inept fool. He was no warrior, he couldn't hunt, and he could barely build a fire. He'd been a failure at "Indianing" since anybody could remember. He went out to the forest, couldn't find a lion or a bear, but did manage to find a sleeping hippopotamus wallowing in the river. He shot it, skinned it, and brought the hippo skin back to camp. The chief was impressed, and he realized that although this was no fierce forest animal, the young brave had fulfilled his hunting obligation.

"Would you like to marry my third, very plain daughter?" the chief asked.

The brave replied that he did.

"Take the hippopotamus skin to your tepee, lay it on the ground, and my daughter will join you and you may consummate your marriage. Tomorrow I shall perform the sacred marriage ceremony."

And the young brave followed instructions.

Oh wonder of wonders! Nine months later, three wonderful events occurred. The first Indian brave and his beautiful wife had a baby boy. The second Indian brave and his beautiful wife had a baby boy. But the bumbling Indian who was good at nothing, and his wife who wasn't much better, had twin boys!

The tribe was amazed—none more than the chief— because twins portended something special in Indian folklore, and nobody could understand how this had happened to the third daughter and third brave. Finally the chief gathered his people around him and said, "I believe I know the reason for this mighty event: remember, the sons of the squaw on the hippopotamus is equal to the sons of the squaws on the other two hides."

ANTIQUES FROM CHAN TEAKS

In San Francisco, there lived an old Chinese man named Chan who had operated an antique store for many years. Lately, he'd been plagued by a series of unexplained but daring thefts during the night. It seemed that each morning when he came in to open the store, he discovered another antique or knickknack missing. He decided to stay up all night, hiding in the store, hoping to discover the intruder.

About three in the morning, the back door slowly opened and the intruder appeared. He was a young boy who was trying to disguise himself by putting a bearskin over his shoulders. Unfortunately, the bearskin was too short to cover his entire body and his unshod feet (to keep down noise) were visible below the coat.

The old Chinese proprietor saw the young boy come in. Just when the boy picked up an old Chinese wooden bowl, Chan jumped up and asked, "Who goes there, boyfoot bear with teak of Chan?"

THE DEEP-SEA DIVE

About ten years ago, a disastrous oil spill occurred off the California coast as a result of some sloppy off-shore drilling. Much marine life was killed, including almost all the area's shellfish. Hundreds of clams died and went to heaven.

There, St. Peter greeted them, told them how sorry he was for their misfortune, and welcomed them to heaven. However, St. Peter singled out one clam who was, unfortunately, not righteous enough to enter heaven. He was sent to "the other place."

The clams were sorry when they realized that their friend Sam would not be joining them in heaven, but they were themselves pleased to have made it.

Sam, meanwhile, quickly became bored in hell. There was very little to do, so he decided to open a nightclub. He hired musicians, dancers, singers, and entertainers, and soon his nightclub was the talk of the town. The other clams, up in heaven where it was much quieter, heard the rollicking sounds of fun from Sam's club, and they begged St. Peter to let them pay a visit to their friend. St. Peter was, of course, reluctant, but they begged and finally he relented...but with a warning: "I want you to take your harps with you so everybody will know that you are from heaven, and I want you back at midnight exactly."

The clams quickly agreed. Toting their harps, they went to Sam's nightclub. They ate, drank, sang, danced, and had such a good time renewing their friendship with Sam and meeting new people at the club that they lost track of time. Minutes before midnight, they realized they had to get back to heaven. In their confused leave-taking, one poor clam forgot his harp.

St. Peter asked him what happened, and he replied, "I left my harp in Sam Clam's disco."

GREAT EXPECTORATIONS

Hockey is a pressure-packed sport, especially professional hockey, which is played with emotional intensity. Fights among players are common and penalties result. Occasionally, the psychological ravages on the players are as career-threatening as the physical injuries many experience. Many players can't handle these pressures.

One player on a professional hockey team vying for the coveted playoffs just couldn't control his temper during games. He would fight continually, and he'd find himself spending too much time in the penalty box. This aggressive behavior is often seen as healthy, but only when the team's best interests are served. When a player starts costing his team victories because of excessive penalties, the fans are not reticent about voicing their disgust. That is exactly what happened to this particular player. He began to hear unmerciful and unforgiving booing from the crowd. He retaliated by playing even more aggressively, but more fights occurred and he spent more time off the ice in the penalty box than on the ice helping his team. Finally, his play became so erratic and the time spent in the penalty box so great that the fans stopped booing and resorted to throwing things at him. At last, they bestowed their ultimate gesture of disgust—they began spitting at him.

The hockey star could stand it no longer. He went to see a psychiatrist. He could handle the booing, he said; and he could handle objects thrown at him. However, he could never effectively cope with the fans spitting at him. His confidence eroded, his skills diminished, and he became entirely ineffective.

He finally retired because the psychiatrist couldn't help him solve the spittle of the rinks.

CUNNING LINGUISTICS

Customs never change in some areas. Oxford University in England clings to traditions, and the clashing of old and new is often humorous. One day, while the old literature professor was crossing the campus, accompanied by four of his fawning students, they encountered three ladies of the evening.

The old don asked his students who these young ladies were, and the students, eager to impress their professor with their linguistic virtuosity, told him.

The first said that they were a "jam of tarts."

The second student offered to describe them as a "pride of loins."

The third student said no, rather they were "a flourish of strumpets."

The fourth eagerly characterized the women as "an essay of Trollopes."

The old don, not to be outdone, said, "No, I think they are merely "an anthology of prose."

ROME SERVICE

We all have to travel, and vampires, too, need their rest and relaxation. "What better place than Rome?" thought Count Dracula, and he immediately packed his bags and set off for a week's visit to the Eternal City.

Tired and hungry after his long journey, he called room service as soon as he arrived at his hotel room. Since nothing on the room-service menu seemed appealing, he simply ordered a sandwich. When the waiter arrived with the sandwich, Dracula quickly grabbed the waiter, bit him hungrily on the neck, drank his blood, and tossed him out the window, where he fell ten stories to land at the feet of an itinerant street singer.

The Count's hunger was great, however, and he decided he needed room service again. He ordered another sandwich, and when it arrived, he immediately grabbed the waiter, bit his neck, drank his blood, and tossed him out the same window. The waiter fell at the feet of the same street singer.

Well, you know how vampires are. They have huge appetites, and Dracula needed more. He then drank the blood from a third waiter and tossed him out the same window.

When the third waiter fell at the feet of the street singer, the singer could only respond by singing, "Drained wops keep falling on my head."

SEND IN THE CLONES

We all seek ways to lessen our ever-increasing work loads. This is particularly true in the field of robotic engineering. An enterprising scientist recently devised a unique solution to his heavy research demands. Unable to procure a grant to hire additional help, this intrepid researcher decided to put his genius and skills to work by creating his own assistant. He labored day and night to develop a robot that looked, sounded, and worked exactly as he himself did. Unfortunately, this precise replication of himself had one significant flaw. It had the foulest mouth the scientist had ever heard. The scientist reprogrammed, rebuilt, tried everything he could, but he couldn't repair this one engineering flaw. On the other hand, the robot worked so efficiently, researched so diligently, and performed its tasks so well that the scientist tried to overlook the problem.

Soon, however, the robot's cursing became an encumbrance to the research scientist's own work. The ever-tolerant scientist decided he had to somehow get rid of the robot. Late one night, he crammed the cursing duplicate of himself into his car and drove to the top of a cliff. His plan, of course, was to throw the body over the steep escarpment. When he was certain nobody was looking, he pulled the cursing, protesting robot from the car and threw him over the edge.

As things always seem to turn out, the scientist was, unfortunately, seen by two policemen who happened to be driving by. They stopped him and were about to arrest him when he protested, "No, you can't arrest me. I didn't kill anybody. That body was not a human; it was a robot I created, a duplicate of myself. But I had to destroy it because it had a foul, cursing, gross mouth."

The policemen were sympathetic, but they said, "We'll still have to arrest you for making an obscene clone fall."

INVASION OF PRIVATE SEA

Marineland and other seaquariums provide wonderful entertainment, but they are also important research centers for marine biologists. Marineland built a new tank and imported about eight dolphins to study their mating habits. The officials would entice the dolphins to mate by feeding them baby sea gulls.

They kept the tank a secret, because they didn't want any curious people, especially youngsters intent on watching only the reproducing dolphins, to interfere with their research. But people snuck in after closing hours. The officials then had to take sterner measures. Around the dolphin tank they dug a moat and put three ferocious lions there to prevent people from coming across to watch the dolphins mate.

But people are smart, and one man thought of a way to satisfy a group of curious people, all intent on watching the dolphins frolic and fornicate. With a dart gun, he shot the three lions with a sleeping potion to drug them and keep them down and asleep long enough so that he and the others could walk across to the dolphin tank. There they began to feed baby sea gulls to the dolphins and watch them mate.

Apparently, the man miscalculated the correct sleeping dosage, because the lions began to stir. When they saw the visitors within their reach, they attacked and mauled them.

Moral: Don't transport young gulls across staid lions for immoral porpoises.

MAKING THE GRADE

All students hope for good grades, and some students will go to any means to achieve them.

A young coed in a philosophy class taught by the renowned Dr. George Reality was having difficulty with the subject matter. She struggled with the course, lost among the discussions of existentialism, Aristotelian logic, and humanism. Finally desperate, she offered to go to bed with the professor in order to get a good grade. The professor agreed.

After the final exam (which she probably didn't have to take), she and Professor Reality made mad, passionate love. As a result of her activities—physical rather than mental—she received an A in the class.

Buoyed by her good fortune, she enrolled in one of Professor Reality's courses the following semester, and she assumed that her extracurricular activities of the previous semester would serve her well this time, also. She was more than annoyed when she received an F in the course.

A friend of hers told her that she should have known that to get an A in that class, she had to come two terms with Reality.

SPOOKED BY THE CAMERA

Haunted houses intrigue all of us. After all, there is nothing more thrilling than coming face to face with creaky doors, strange noises, and the possibility of confronting a ghost. However, one young man wanted proof of his visit to a famous haunted house, and he took a camera with him, hoping to photograph a ghost if he saw one.

Sure enough, the spooks were about that night, and the young man saw a ghost in one of the bedrooms of the haunted mansion. He asked the ghost if he could take his picture, and the ghost readily agreed. The young man set up his camera, got the agreeable ghost to pose, and took the picture...but his camera malfunctioned and the bulb failed to work.

Obviously, the spirit was willing but the flash was weak.

HARES TO PARIS

The French will eat almost anything. (Perhaps that's why they had to learn to make wine, but that's another story.) A young cook decided that the French would enjoy feasting on rabbits, and he decided to raise rabbits in Paris and sell them to the restaurants in the city.

He searched all over Paris seeking a suitable place to raise his rabbits. None could be found. Finally, an old priest at the cathedral said he could have a small area behind the rectory for his rabbits.

He successfully raised a number of them and when he went about Paris selling them, a restaurant owner asked him where he got such fresh rabbits. The young man replied, "I raise them myself, near the cathedral. In fact, I have a hutch back of Notre Dame."

MARTIAN TO A DIFFERENT DRUMMER

What's out there, in the far reaches of outer space? The American space probes are trying to find out, but few people know that one of America's space missions did discover a form of life...on Mars.

The manned expedition landed on Mars; and as soon as the astronauts disembarked from their space ship, they were met by hundreds of little furry balls with short, little legs. The little furries, as they were called, were very polite and cooperative, and when the leader of the space expedition asked some of the furry balls to take them to their leader, the furries began to lead them.

The astronauts were amazed to see that the population of Mars consisted almost entirely of these little furries going about their business. After walking for several hours, the astronauts saw a large furry, twice the size of the others, sitting on a hill with what appeared to be a hypodermic needle sticking out from its head. The astronauts asked, "Is that your leader?"

The furry ball leading them said, "No, that's just the furry with the syringe on top."

CHAIR THE WEALTH

A remote group of natives lives in the darkest reaches of unexplored Africa. Word got out that this was a rich tribe, with much wealth garnered from the precious stones in the area. In fact, the king of the tribe had a beautiful throne made from rare wood and decorated with beautiful precious stones which he kept in his thatched-roof hut.

When other tribes heard about this throne, they were intent on stealing it from the king and becoming rich. One day the king heard from his messengers that an armed group was approaching the tribe's village, and the king could only assume they were coming to steal his valuable throne. He immediately took steps to hide it. With the help of other tribesmen, he hid the throne in the rafters of his hut, hoping that the men coming to steal it wouldn't find it.

Unfortunately, the primitive hut couldn't support the weight of the throne, and it crashed down, destroying the hut and injuring the king. Needless to say, the throne was lost to the bounty seekers.

Moral: Those who live in grass houses shouldn't stow thrones.

DO THE RIGHT SING

A friend of mine told me about some experiences he once had while serving as a counselor at a camp for retarded children. The camp had many of the same activities one would find at any camp: baseball, swimming, crafts, and so forth. One of the activities my friend was responsible for was directing the camp glee club.

But he had his troubles. The retarded campers wouldn't cooperate; they didn't want to sing. So my friend bribed them. He told them that if they sang and learned the songs, he would give them snacks. The campers liked this idea, and their singing improved as they were bribed with candy, potato chips, pretzels, and assorted junk food.

The camp director found out about this and was worried. After all, he felt, these kids needed exercise and good food in order to have a healthy summer camp experience. He confronted the glee club director and told him, "We have enough trouble trying to keep these kids healthy. When you feed them junk food, they only get fat."

"What should I do?" asked my friend. "This is the only way I can get them to sing."

The camp director suggested giving them health foods like juices and fruits. "Why not give them oranges and apples, or diet drinks and juices?"

My friend tried this, and he was successful. From that moment on, the camp glee club was known as the Moron Tab and Apple Choir.

DARNED TOOTIN'

A man suffering from the most embarrassing intestinal problem visited his internist to try to end his constant gas problems. It seemed that he continually passed gas; and what made the problem more embarrassing was the loud sound it made. For some reason, his passing gas sounded like a loud motorcycle's exhaust.

He went from doctor to doctor, from specialist to specialist. After dozens of tests, a stomach specialist told him the problem was caused by an abcess. The man couldn't understand the diagnosis.

"How is that possible? How can an abcess cause me to pass gas that sounds like a motorcycle exhaust?"

The doctor replied, "Abcess makes the fart go Honda."

HAVING A FEW POPS

During an outdoor concert one summer, the Boston Pops was scheduled to perform Beethoven's Ninth Symphony. Three bass singers, realizing that they didn't have to perform until the end of the piece, decided to slip out early during the first few movements and have a few beers. Because it was a windy day, they secured their music to their stands with some twine and went to a nearby tavern, planning to return when they had to sing.

As luck would have it, they enjoyed their drinking so much they lost track of time and were late returning to perform. When they did return, they were in no condition to sing. The conductor was exasperated. In fact, he was so upset that he stopped the performance, snapped his baton in two, and angrily left the stage.

The stage manager was mortified and ran after him, asking why he had left the concert so abruptly. The conductor stopped, whirled around, and exclaimed, "Well, what would you do? It's the last of the ninth, the score is tied, and the basses are loaded."

A PITCHER FULL OF BEER

It was the seventh game of the World Series, and everything was riding on the usually sure but occasionally erratic arm of young pitcher Mel Famey. He was scheduled to pitch the deciding game, and his manager knew everything would be all right as long as they could keep Mel from having one or two or three too many beers before the game. When Mel drank, he tended to get wild.

The opposing manager knew this also, and he sent two of his players to try to get Mel to imbibe a few the night before the game. These two henchmen succeeded in dragging Mel to a local tavern where, sure enough, Mel couldn't resist the temptation of the suds. To be on the safe side, the two opposing players brought along an extra six-pack and stowed it in Mel's locker, hoping he might even have a few more before or during the game.

When the game was about to begin, Mel Famey's manager took one look at Mel's inebriated condition and wouldn't let him start; instead, he relegated Mel to the bullpen. There he languished until the ninth inning. The score was tied, but the opposition had the bases loaded. Mel's manager had no choice; Mel was his only available pitcher. Mel came in to pitch the bottom of the ninth inning...and promptly pitched wildly and walked in the winning run.

The two opposing players stole into Mel's locker to remove any evidence of wrongdoing by taking back the beer. They showed it to their teammates with this comment: "Here's the beer that made Mel Famey walk us."

HEALTH TO THE CHIEF

An Indian chief was suffering from a serious stomach disorder. His pains were excruciating, and he turned to the tribe's medicine man to see if something could be done.

The medicine man practiced his traditional arts: he danced around the chief singing ancient songs, he burned incense, and he tried to frighten the demons and pains away with his ugly masks. Finally, he gave the chief a 30-inch strip of buffalo hide to chew on. The chief's instructions were to take one bite a day until the leather strip was gone.

After thirty days, the medicine man asked the chief how he was feeling. The still-ailing chief replied, "The thong is ended, but the malady lingers on."

SCRAPPY TRAILS TO YOU

A few years ago, it seems some cougars were getting into the corral where Roy Rogers' and Dale Evans' horses were kept, frightening and panicking the horses. Roy decided to go out and hunt down the marauding cougars.

He hadn't been out hunting in years, and had nothing to wear. Dale presented him with a new trousseau, a hunting outfit complete with new boots. Roy went out to the corral, saddled up Trigger, and went riding out into cougar territory.

Just as he rode beneath a tree, a cougar jumped down from the branches and grabbed Roy by the boot. The cougar tore and twisted, but Roy managed to subdue it. He tied the cougar behind him and rode back to the ranch.

Dale took one look at Roy's torn boots and the dead cougar and exclaimed, "Pardon me, Roy, is that the cat who chewed your new shoes?"

THEIR FATE WAS SEALED

Two eskimos set out to hunt the fur-bearing seals of the Arctic. They loaded their small, two-man canoe with all the gear they'd need and sailed out into the cold ocean waters.

Their hunt was very successful—so successful, in fact, that the boat was overladen with seals and sealskins. They had to throw many of their supplies away in order to stash their rich cache of furs.

On the way back to the village, they encountered a fierce storm. In order to survive, they knew they'd have to build a fire to keep warm; but they had thrown all their fuel out of the boat.

Nevertheless, they managed to build a small fire in the craft, but the fire blew out of control, sinking the boat and causing the loss of all furs. The eskimos learned a valuable lesson: You can't have your kayak and heat it too.

SOUNDS FISHY TO ME

Civilization comes to everybody eventually, whether they like it or not. It certainly happened to the Indians who lived along the east coast of the United States.

At one time, these Indians procured most of their food by fishing. They'd fish the rivers, streams, and ocean, never failing to reap a bountiful harvest from the local waters.

But one day a man who sold bicycles came to the Indian village and convinced the Indians that they would be safer and catch more fish if they fished from bicycles rather than take their chances in their rickety canoes. This idea raised much dissension among the Indians. After all, they had fished from boats for hundreds—no, thousands—of years. Why change now?

The chief suggested they have a contest, with some Indians fishing from bicycles and others from canoes. The tribe agreed; and when the results were counted, it was evident that using the bicycles was more efficient—those on the bicycles caught more fish. From then on each Indian fished from a bicycle rather than a canoe because his barque was worse than his bike.

AN ARRESTING CASE

A young policeman on his beat was very surprised one night to see his former supervisor, the lieutenant, also pounding a beat at night. He asked him what he was doing. After all, this was not the sort of duty a lieutenant usually performs.

The former lieutenant replied that last week he had arrested a judge who was on his way to a masquerade ball, dressed as a criminal, complete with mask. "How could I tell it was a judge dressed for a costume party?" the former lieutenant said.

The young cop nodded sympathetically, saying, "Yes, it's wise never to book a judge by his cover."

SOUTHERN DISCOMFORT

Before the Civil War, a rich Southern gentleman owned an ironworks where he manufactured boilers, kettles, and stoves. Being the entrepreneur that he was, he did a little slave trading on the side. He kept his slaves in the basement of his factory, just beneath the area where his stovemakers worked.

One day the boss brought in a slave whom he was about to sell, but the slave was very sick; in fact, he had a temperature of 105 degrees. The sick slave was delirious, ranting all day, making it difficult for the stovemakers above him to work.

Finally the day ended, and a frustrated, tired stover returned home. His wife looked at him and remarked how tired he looked.

"You'd be tired too," he replied, "if you'd been stoving over a hot slave all day."

WE DO IT ALL FOR EWES

During a very cold winter's night, a shepherd sent his two sons up to the high pasture, many miles from their house, to make certain the sheep were not suffering from the cold. The two young shepherds trudged out reluctantly, and when they reached the pasture, one was so tired he would not go into the pasture to check the sheep. The other dutifully spent most of the night rounding up sheep and herding them into a corral.

The next night, the father journeyed up to the high pasture to check on his sons and the sheep. He found his dutiful son asleep. Asking him how he felt, the son replied that he was cold and tired from working all night, and his lamp had gone out. The father, proud of his loyal, hard-working son, gave him oil and a wick for his lamp.

When the father checked on his other son, he found him soundly sleeping. Upon waking him, he asked how he was, and the son replied that he was cold because his lamp had gone out. When he asked for a new lamp, his father replied, "You can have no lamp. There is no wick for the rested."

A FLAGON THE PLAY

The coach of a college football team was having a problem with some of his players. Most adhered strictly to training rules, but a few would take advantage of the welcoming taverns in the town and occasionally sneak some drinks.

One night, the coach, anxious because some of his players were missing during bedcheck, made the rounds of the local pubs in search of his players. Just as he entered one bar, two of his star players, the quarterback and fullback, spotted him and tried to sneak off into the lavatory.

The bartender asked the coach what he wanted to drink, and the coach replied, "Just a Coke for me, but see what the backs in the boys' room will have."

AFRICAN VIOLENCE

A small country in central Africa depended on hunting safaris for its livelihood. The country grew very rich as American and European hunters came to the country, and they paid princely fees to hunt in the game-rich country.

However, a new king decided that hunting was a cruel sport, and he immediately outlawed hunting. The absence of rich hunters began to plague the country in many ways: no money came into the kingdom, and the wild animals began to proliferate. Lions, snakes, and other wild beasts became more than a nuisance; they were overrunning the villages and endangering the people.

Finally, the people had had enough. They overthrew the king and his government and brought back the hunters. This was the one instance in history of a reign being cancelled on account of the game.

WATER DO THINK OF THAT?

During an anthropology class at Columbia University, two students became very interested in how the ancient Egyptians managed to irrigate that dry country. They decided to visit Egypt to try to determine how the Egyptians drew water from the Nile.

They went off to Egypt where they found out that the same methods used over two thousand years ago were still in place. They began examining the pipes, ducts, and sewers of the city. They even examined the bathroom facilities in the public buildings.

When they returned, they decided to change their course of study from anthropology and become pharoah faucet majors.

BOOTY IS ONLY SKIN DEEP

Avoiding the traumas of old age and trying to be forever young has always been a human quest. How else do we explain the billion dollars a year spent on vanishing creams, face lifts, and other assorted "youth" formulas?

One of the most successful purveyors of cosmetics designed to keep people looking young and healthy was an entrepreneurial dermatologist named Dr. Lisa. In fact, Dr. Lisa's advertisements promised that women in their forties could take twenty-five to thirty years off their lives and have skin like sixteen-year-olds if they used her skin formulas.

And these formulas worked. Millions of Americans began using Dr. Lisa's cosmetics and looking younger. Dr. Lisa was so popular and famous as the owner of a very large, successful cosmetic empire that she was encouraged to run for public office because of the influence she had over millions of women.

It was said, of course, that what would elect her to office would be the teening power of Lisa.

JUST DESSERTS

William Penn is, of course, famous as the founder of the Pennsylvania Commonwealth and leader of the Quakers who settled that important area of America. What many people don't know is that William Penn was not the only famous Penn in Philadelphia. In fact, Penn had two aunts who sparked an economic revolution of their own.

Williams Penn's two aunts were in the bakery business, and they were famous for their pies—especially their apple cobblers and cherry pies. However, the competition in old Philadelphia was brutal, and the other bakers bound together to try to force the two women out of business. The other bakers lowered their prices, but the two ladies lowered theirs even more. In fact, good William's aunts lowered their prices so much (and they still baked the best pies in Philadelphia), that many of the other bakers were forced out of business.

All over Philadelphia, there was talk of little else but the pie rates of Penn's aunts.

BEEF FARE TO YOUR NEIGHBOR

A butcher in New York swears that this story is true. He had a flourishing business next to an exclusive apartment building in which a lot of United Nations representatives lived. One of the representatives was a mysterious mystic from India who continually berated the butcher for selling beef. Cattle, of course, were sacred in this mystic's Hindu religion.

One day, up in his apartment, the mystic became very ill. The doctor, after examining him, prescribed some meat for his diet; in fact he suggested that beef liver might be the best diet supplement the sick man could have. The mystic reluctantly agreed that his health was too important to jeopardize, so he went down to the butcher to order some. The butcher, realizing his chance to get back at the man for all his insults, decided to overcharge him by lying to him about the weight of the meat.

He told his assistant, "When you put his purchase on the scale, press down with your thumb on the scale in order to weigh down upon the swami's liver."

LOSS AT SEA

Anybody who has ever gone deep-sea fishing knows how strenuous that sport can be. Once you've hooked one of those big fish, you can be fighting him for hours. Occasionally you lose your concentration in the struggle.

A man went down to Florida and hired a fishing boat to take him out fishing for marlin. Sure enough, he hooked a big one and the two began fighting each other for hours. Suddenly, the marlin gave a tug on the line, jerking the man so powerfully that his billfold flew right out of his shirt pocket and into the ocean.

Incredibly, it was caught by a fish swimming on the surface, and the fish, in a playful mood, tossed it to one of his companions. They continued to toss the billfold back and forth in an amazing display of piscatorial dexterity.

In fact, this was the first instance of carp-to-carp walleting.

WEATHER YOU LIKE IT OR NOT

One of the most famous media stars in the Soviet Union was Rudolf Minsky, the famous weatherman. Whenever Russians were planning an outing or some type of outdoor event whose success depended on the weather, they always listened intently to Rudolf's weather forecast—he was rarely wrong.

A young man working in the ministry of planning was trying to interest young Olga to go out with him. He planned a picnic, but when he finally asked her, she said no, because according to Rudolf Minsky, showers were expected that day. The young man persisted, and he finally convinced young Olga to accompany him on the picnic.

They took a bus to the outskirts of Moscow, hiked to a park, and settled down to eat their lunch. Suddenly, it began to shower.

"I told you there would be showers," said Olga. "You should listen to me. After all, Rudolf the Red knows rain, dear."

THE SMARTY BOAT

The Spanish government decided to honor all recent Nobel
Prize winners with a reception and conference in Barcelona.
The Spanish government invited almost one hundred Nobel
Prize winners to come to Spain and live on a luxury yacht
anchored in the Mediterranean off the coast near Barcelona.
Almost all the invitees accepted.

During their first night on the boat, the Nobel Prize
winners were so taken by each other's company, the
sparkling and intelligent conversation, and the stimulating
exchange of ideas, that they didn't want to leave the boat for
the dinner in their honor. They insisted that they enjoyed
being out on the ocean with each other. They made their
point quite adamantly...they did not want to leave each
other's company on the boat.

This was obviously a case where the brains in Spain
stayed plainly on the main.

UNCLE AT FAULT

A young boy was very excited when his uncle promised to take him to the circus one day. The boy looked forward to the outing for several weeks, but when the day of the circus visit came, his uncle was nowhere to be found.

"Where's Uncle Alfred?" the boy asked his mother. "He was supposed to take me to the circus today." His mother replied that Uncle Al must have forgotten, because he had gone to London to see the Wimbledon matches.

"I didn't know Uncle Alfred liked tennis," said the boy.

"Oh yes," replied his mother, "in fact, he talks about it all the time. I have often heard Alfred laud tennis, son."

HOW TO MAKE MORE BREAD

A young man worked in a bakery and earned his living cutting bread. In fact, he was paid on the basis of how many loaves of bread he could cut in a day. It didn't take this young man long to realize that if he got himself a longer knife, he might be able to cut two loaves of bread at the same time and earn twice as much money as previously. He bought himself a longer knife and sure enough, he was cutting two loaves of bread in the time it used to take him to cut one.

After a few weeks of earning twice the money as before, he realized that he could get himself an even longer knife and cut three loaves of bread and earn three times the money he had originally earned.

Such experience was not lost on him, and he began to search for a very long knife that could cut four loaves of bread at one time. Such knives are not easy to locate, and he spent many weeks, even months, searching throughout the country for an appropriate knife.

At last he found a knife long enough to suit his needs. He celebrated. He jumped and danced through the streets to celebrate his good fortune. A friend saw him and commented on how happy he looked.

"Of course I'm happy," replied the young bread cutter. "Today is my lucky day—I just found a four-loaf cleaver."

BULLY FOR YOU

A small village at the foot of a mountain was experiencing some unfortunate violence. The village, inhabited by peace-loving Trids, was bothered occasionally by a mean ogre who lived on the mountain. The ogre, to satisfy his violent nature, would periodically come down from the mountain at night, enter the village, and find some unsuspecting Trid to torment and beat up. The ogre's favorite form of fighting consisted of kicking the poor Trid into senselessness.

After years of this violence, the Trids decided they'd had enough. The town council met and elected a representative from the town's elders to confront the ogre and try to persuade him to stop kicking the Trids. The council elected the town rabbi as emissary.

The rabbi hiked up the mountain to discuss the situation with the ogre. When he got there, he presented his case: "Why do you insist on beating up the harmless Trids?" asked the rabbi.

The ogre replied that this was his favorite form of recreation and he had to beat up somebody.

The rabbi replied, "Why pick on the small Trids? If you must kick somebody, fight me."

The ogre replied that he couldn't do that: "Silly rabbi, kicks are for Trids."

NUT WHAT I ORDERED

Old Dr. Smith had the habit of going into the bar next to his office and enjoying a daiquiri each morning before meeting his patients. He had gotten into this habit during medical school training in the Caribbean, and he had fallen in love with that tangy lime flavor. The lime daiquiri just seemed to hit the spot and get him off on the right foot each day.

Unfortunately, a citrus blight had destroyed most of Florida's lime crop one year, and taverns began searching for substitutes with which to prepare their daiquiris. Dr. Smith's favorite tavern experimented with berries, herbs, nuts, and other ingredients, and they were most successful using the pressings and oozings of hickory nuts.

Of course, knowing how much their most faithful customer depended on his lime daiquiri each morning, they always gave him one, as long as there was a lime to be found in town.

But the day finally came when there were no limes to be found in town, and the bartender had to hand Dr. Smith one of his experiments. The good doctor took a sip of his eye-opener, and his eyes popped wide open. "This isn't my drink," he exclaimed. "What is it?"

The bartender replied, "No, it's not. It's a hickory daiquiri, Doc."

IF YOU KNEW SUSHI

Although many people still blanch and hesitate when considering sampling sushi, Japanese restaurants are increasing rapidly as more and more people partake of these delicacies. Tuna, eel, salmon, clam, octopus, and other raw treasures from the sea are becoming more and more popular. One of the new taste sensations at sushi restaurants these days is an unusual fish called the luchu.

The luchu is not served as other sushi dishes are; rather, it is served with ceremony and flair worthy of the exquisite care and beauty the Japanese give many of their dishes. Perhaps it is because the luchu fish contains a poison gland that must be carefully removed before the fish is served. The sushi chef carefully, but with elaborate ceremony, prepares the fish in front of his customers, carefully cutting out the poison gland and ceremoniously shaping the fish. Custom demands that the luchu be cut into small, precise square pieces. After cutting out the poison gland, the chef is ready to cut the fish into cubes.

At this point, when the fish is to be cut and served, the chef announces with a flourish: "We who are about to dice a luchu."

ART OF MY ART

A young couple, Wilbur and Kay, were exploring the Art Institute of Chicago one Sunday afternoon when they came upon the museum's famous collection of Eighteenth-Century French art. Suddenly Wilbur, unfamiliar as he was with the fine points of the period, came upon a well-known painting he mistakenly thought was an example of pointillism. He immediately called his wife over and naively exclaimed, "Kay, Seurat, Seurat!"

She took one bored look at the painting and replied, "Whatever, Wilby, Wilby."